Arachnids

Level 10 – White

Helpful Hints for Reading at Home

The graphemes (written letters) and phonemes (units of sound) used throughout this series are aligned with Letters and Sounds. This offers a consistent approach to learning whether reading at home or in the classroom.

HERE ARE SOME COMMON WORDS THAT YOUR CHILD MIGHT FIND TRICKY:

water	where	would	know	thought	through	couldn't
laughed	eyes	once	we're	school	can't	our

TOP TIPS FOR HELPING YOUR CHILD TO READ:

- Encourage your child to read aloud as well as silently to themselves.
- Allow your child time to absorb the text and make comments.
- Ask simple questions about the text to assess understanding.
- Encourage your child to clarify the meaning of new vocabulary.

This book focuses on developing independence, fluency and comprehension. It is a White level 10 book band.

©2022 **BookLife Publishing Ltd.**
King's Lynn, Norfolk PE30 4LS

ISBN 978–1–80155–113–7

All rights reserved. Printed in Poland.
A catalogue record for this book is available from the British Library.

Arachnids
Written by Joanna Brundle
Adapted by Robin Twiddy
Designed by Gareth Liddington

Image Credits Images are courtesy of Shutterstock.com. With thanks to Getty Images, Thinkstock Photo and iStockphoto. Cover – Peratek, ClassicVector, Olga Kovalenko, Pisut, Torychemistry, varuna. p4–5 –Alex Stemmer, Yuvan aves. p6–7 –Audrey Snider-Bell, torook. p8–9 – Kurt Hohenbichler, Paul Looyen. p10–11 – Art Wittingen, Kopiyka. p12–13 – LorraineHudgins, Tom Wurl. p14–15 –Henrik Larsson, Ian Scammell. p16–17 – Gabi Wolf, Henrik Larsson. p18–19 – Joy Ondreicka, guentermanaus. p20–21 – Lamyai, Alex Stemmer, stevenku.

Contents

Arachnids

Arachnids have been around for 400 million years and inhabit every continent on Earth except Antarctica. It is estimated that there are 90,000 species of arachnid, including spiders, crabs and scorpions. Arachnids live in all kinds of habitat, including forests, deserts, rainforests, swamps and mountains.

Unlike insects, which have six legs and three segments to their bodies, arachnids have eight legs and two segments: a head and an abdomen. Most arachnids lay eggs, but scorpions give birth to live young.

ARACHNID CHECKLIST
- No backbone
- Cold-blooded
- Most lay eggs
- Two body segments
- Eight legs
- Exoskeleton (skeleton outside the body)

Body Parts

Exoskeleton

Arachnids have a hard outer layer called an exoskeleton, which supports and protects them from the outside, rather than the inside. An exoskeleton cannot get bigger so, as an arachnid grows, it produces a new, larger exoskeleton and moults out of the old one.

Legs

Arachnids have jointed legs. The exoskeleton is stiff and cannot bend, so jointed legs help an arachnid to move quickly and skilfully. Arachnids have 48 knees – six on each of their eight legs! If a leg is broken, a new one grows between moults.

Tarantula

Spinnerets

Spiders have organs called spinnerets on the underside of their abdomens. They use spinnerets to spin silk. The silk is squeezed out through tiny holes in the spinnerets. In the air, the silk becomes sticky and is used to make webs and cocoons for eggs.

Wasp spider's spinneret weaving a web

The Front Segment

The front segment of an arachnid's body contains the animal's eyes, stomach, brain, mouth, fangs and venom glands. All eight legs are attached to the front segment.

Spiders usually have eight eyes, but most have very poor eyesight.

Getting Around

Arachnids move about by walking, running, jumping and even swimming. Spiders move using hydraulics. This means that they use liquid under pressure to create power where it is needed. While two pairs of legs are in the air, the other two pairs are on the ground for support.

Raft spiders can walk on water.

Spiders can run up walls and across ceilings thanks to over 500,000 tiny hairs called setules, found on the ends of its legs.

Some spiders travel by ballooning. This is when a spider climbs very high and then releases lots of silk into the wind, which carries the spider.

Predators and Prey

Most arachnids eat other animals. Spiders eat a variety of insects, while tarantulas eat frogs, mice and birds. Larger tarantulas also eat lizards, bats and small snakes. Spiders can last weeks without food.

This garden spider has caught a monarch butterfly in its web.

Animals that hunt spiders include monkeys, birds and centipedes. The tarantula hawk, which is actually a wasp, is a predator that hunts tarantulas in their burrows. It paralyses the tarantula with a sting, then drags it to its own burrow to feed its young.

A tarantula hawk with its paralysed prey

Adaptation

Arachnids have adapted to their environments in many amazing ways. Adaptation helps a species to survive by enabling animals to cope with extreme conditions and warding off predators. Crab spiders can camouflage themselves by changing colour to match their environment.

This goldenrod crab spider is perfectly camouflaged on a dandelion.

Most scorpions live in hot, dry areas of desert. Scorpions have adapted to live in this environment. Food is hard to come by in the desert, so scorpions have adapted to be able to go without food for up to a year!

This emperor scorpion is eating its prey.

Life Cycles

Before mating, male arachnids do special things. For example, this might involve special movements, such as rocking their bodies back and forth. A male spider pulls on the female's web in a particular way, so that she knows he is a mate, rather than her dinner!

Female spiders are much bigger than male spiders and often eat the male after mating.

Almost all female spiders spin an egg sac out of silk to protect their eggs. Some hide the egg sac under a rock or attach it to a plant. Some species carry the egg sac on their bodies. These spiderlings then ride on their mother's back until they are ready to leave her.

Egg sac

Extreme Arachnids

Black Widow Spider

Black widow spiders are some of the most venomous spiders the world. The females have a red or orange hourglass shape on their abdomen, while males have red or pink spots. Their bite is thought to be 15 times more venomous than a rattlesnake's.

Goliath Birdeater

The Goliath birdeater is the largest spider in the world by weight. It can defend itself by rubbing the hairs on its body together to make a hissing sound. It can also send out a shower of spiked hairs from its abdomen that ward off predators.

Female Goliath birdeaters can live for up to 20 years.

Emperor Scorpion

The emperor scorpion has hairs on its pincers and tail. These hairs pick up vibrations in the air and on the ground, helping the scorpion to discover prey. Scorpions glow a bluish green under UV light. Scientists think this glow may ward off predators but also attract insects as prey.

Dust Mites

Although we cannot see them, dust mites share our homes with us. Every 24 hours, the average human loses 1 million dead skin cells. These cells provide food for dust mites. Dust mites suck water out of the air, so humid places make ideal habitats.

Dust mite

Index

eyes 9
heads 5
legs 5, 7, 9–11
mites 21
scorpions 4–5, 15, 20

spiders 4, 8–14, 16–19
spinnerets 8
webs 8, 12, 16

How to Use an Index

An index helps us to find information in a book. Each word has a set of page numbers. These page numbers are where you can find information about that word.

Page numbers

Example: balloons 5, 8–10, 19

Important word

This means page 8, page 10, and all the pages in between. Here, it means pages 8, 9 and 10.

Questions

1. How many legs do arachnids have?

2. What is the largest spider in the world by weight?

3. What are baby spiders called?

4. Can you use the contents page to find out about how arachnids get around?

5. Can you use the index page to find dust mites in the book?